Chapters

Introduction

OUR original plan was to produce a book focussing on the huge number of Routemasters that continue to generate revenue sixty years after the first one appeared on London streets. Once the picture search began, though, it soon became obvious that the same could be said about the RT family, the RFs, the GSs, even the surviving RLHs, to name but a few.

One hasty re-think later, we came up with **London's Working Heritage**, featuring a much wider selection of older types engaged in revenue-earning activity . . . or perhaps merely working.

At least one of us would argue that re-creating a route counts as 'working', because that's what the bus was originally built to do. The fact that many of these activities have souvenir programmes attached, which passengers have to buy to gain access to the 'free' rides, proves that revenue takes many forms.

Within these pages, you will find London vehicles raising money for charity, fulfilling commercial contracts, providing sightseeing tours, dispensing beer and chips, or any of a myriad of other activities where cash is extracted from pockets, wallets or bank accounts.

The definition of 'heritage', of course, depends entirely on when you were born, and we have tried to take that into account.

We must thank the photographers who've supplied material for the book, especially those who came up with the shots we didn't have, or were able to illustrate rarer subjects like the Canadian Clan.

We've also had a huge amount of help from a select band of individuals engaged in the day-to-day running of the vehicles shown here. Our special thanks to them.

Ken Carr   Picture sourcing, research, design and layout
David Maxey   Text

May 2014

Cover Picture: Ensign's Wartime Tour of London has proved immensely popular, with a member of the RT family appearing every day the trip runs, alongside RMs when demand is high. RTL453 is a regular performer. *Brian Kemp*

Frontispiece: Hiring a bus for a wedding continues to grow in popularity. Here, for instance, Dulcie and BIll celebrate their special day with Routemaster Hire's RML2374. *Peter Horrex*

Below: RML2683, on the other hand, may have been on a secret mission. No-one knows why it appeared on private hire duty in Brentford in April 2014. *Jack Marian*

Back Cover: The Commissioner's RM1005 at St George's Square, Pimlico, during the running day celebrating route 24's centenary, 15th March 2013. *David Maxey*

Heritage Route 15 was introduced in November 2005, one month before Routemasters' final day in front-line service. It runs between two London icons - the Tower of London and Trafalgar Square. Along its route it passes a third - the 300-year-old St Paul's Cathedral. RM2071 poses beneath the famous dome. *Ken Carr*

After dropping off passengers at the last stop by the Tower of London, the 15's RMs proceed to their dedicated stand in Goodman's Yard. RM2071, again, is passed by Abellio's Dart Pointer 8304 on the meandering route 100. In the background, the viaduct supports the electrified main line from Fenchurch Street to Essex. *David Maxey*

Winding back a quarter-of-a-mile, RM1968 approaches the final stop, which is also close by Tower Hill Underground station. Here, the backdrop is provided by 10 Trinity Square, once the Headquarters of the Port of London Authority. You may recognise it from a recent James Bond film. *David Maxey*

Because the 15H is a 15-minute interval service, you need to be lucky to capture two together. In one such lucky moment, this is RM652 heading east past RM1933 at the junction of Byward Street and Lower Thames Street.

1933 is approaching the unusual 'bus gate' featured in a *Streets of London* DVD. *David Maxey*
Below: A selection of close-ups from a West Ham garage visit. *Ken Carr*

RM2060 heads around the Aldwych crescent, closely followed by an Enviro400 hybrid working the regular route 15. In September 2013, when this shot was taken, the 'proper' 15 was also terminating at Trafalgar Square. *Ken Carr*

Old and new in the Strand: RM1968 is followed by LT52 outside the Strand Palace Hotel. In the far distance, you can just make out Nelson's Column, where the heritage 15s begin their eastbound journey. Once an all-RM route itself, the 11 converted to the LT type in August 2013. *Ken Carr*

Both 15s sometimes terminate westbound at Aldwych, usually at weekends when the Strand is closed for building work. RM2060 is standing on the spot normally occupied by route 6, 9 & 87 vehicles at the end of their journeys. *David Maxey*

The 15H's western stand is in Great Scotland Yard, which forms part of a loop from Northumberland Avenue into Whitehall before regaining line of route at Trafalgar Square. The stand is shared with the other heritage service, the 9H, which appears later in the book, as does the silver RM1650. *David Maxey*

Weekend diversions are a regular hazard in the City of London, so the 15s are often caught up in them. This one via Waterloo, however, is rare and must have arisen from a blockage of Fleet Street *and* the Embankment. RM652 strays perilously close to a different Stagecoach company. *David Maxey*

A westbound blockage in Fleet Street diverted all routes via Victoria Embankment on a weekend in March 2014. RM2089 swings off the Blackfriars bridge approach road with, left to right, The Gherkin, The Cheesegrater and The Walkie-Talkie as the background scenery. The construction resembling a car park nearer the camera is the new Blackfriars main line station straddling the Thames. *David Maxey*

From the same West Ham visit, a partial line-up of the ten-strong RM allocation during the morning run-out. Three have already left, the other two are in the maintenance shed. The first of the daily allocation leaves the garage at 08.56, the last at 09.39. *David Maxey*

A slightly different view of the RMs at West Ham. It could almost be the 1960s . . . apart from the yellow trims. *Ken Carr*

RM324 is the oldest of the Stagecoach RMs. It entered service from Shepherd's Bush garage in July 1960 when trolleybus routes 628 & 630 converted. Despite trips to Aldenham for overhaul, a bus with this number always found its way back to 'the Bush' and stayed there for 34 years.

How much of the original RM324 survives today is a matter of conjecture, but it's an interesting 'number' all the same. Here, WLT324 is about to start another day's work from the East London base after collecting a conductor from the admin block at the far end of the shed. *David Maxey*

And finally, RM1968 sets out as the last of the five vehicles on that particular day. This, of course, is the modern West Ham, completed in June 2010. The original West Ham garage in Greengate Street, Plaistow, was built as a tram depot in 1906 and closed in 1992. *David Maxey*

Advertising & Corporate Capers

BECAUSE Routemasters are instantly noticed by the general public, advertisers find them irresistible as mobile billboards. Whether you approve or disapprove is irrelevant because such use generates revenue and helps to keep more examples running.

Painting one pink, though, may be a step too far. RML2628's operator, Blush Hospitality, specialises in Hen Nights, hence the awful colour because girlies like pink. According to the company website, the Blushbus has been "refitted lavishly to a breath-taking standard" and is "a chic and exclusive vehicle". A more pithy description is "ruined". The photographer wishes to remain anonymous.

For the 2012 London Olympics, Russian sportswear manufacturer Bosco hired three Routemasters from Ensignbus to promote its brand. Three teams would be wearing Bosco kit at the Games - Russia, Ukraine and Spain - so a bus was created for each.

A fortnight before the opening ceremony, Ensign began transforming the vehicles at its Purfleet workshops. RML2516 was the first to receive the 'understated' vinyls, in the design representing Ukraine. *Ken Carr*

Bottom of page: Once all three were finished, an impromptu photo shoot was arranged. Left to right, RM371 (Spain), RCL2220 (Russia) and RML2516 line up on 28th July before heading into Central London, where they were used by Bosco officials and guests throughout the Games. *Bob Stanger*

The slightly confused message on RML2545 reflects the tie-up between Keds Sneakers and American singer-songwriter Taylor Swift. So the vinyls mostly mention The Red Tour to promote her new album in 2014. What the bus is doing in Euston Road is anyone's guess. *David Maxey*

RML2757 provides slightly more obvious advertising outside The Avenue shopping centre in Spinningfields, Manchester. The Manchester Duck Race is held every Easter and involves the setting free of thousands of rubber ducks into the River Irwell. And why not? *Mike Williams*

RML2464 has been converted into a mobile bank by NatWest and in April 2013 turned up at Tooting Broadway. Since then, it's been repainted into a dark blue corporate livery and has appeared at locations all over Britain. You may prefer to remember it working route 94 for London United. *Brian Kemp*

RML2558 received a white base coat in 2010 and appeared at the Epsom Derby as Investec's 'Zebra Bus'. Just before Christmas 2011, it reappeared with Samsung vinyls to promote the new NX200 camera system. This is a lunchtime break in Cockspur Street near Trafalgar Square. *David Maxey*

RCL2240, owned by Wells Brewery, is used to promote its Bombardier real ale. In July 2012 it took part in the Bedford River Fesival and gained its own police escort. *Albert Dawson*

RCL2250 spent a number of years advertising (and dispensing) Corona beer. The bus visited Wimbledon for the 2009 All England Tennis Championships complete with an out-of-work actor dressed as a bottle of beer 'upstairs'. Luckily there aren't any low bridges between Wimbledon station and Centre Court.

More recently, the bus has been bought by On The Green of Kingsbridge, Devon and is now in use as a mobile cafe, repainted in Lincoln Green. *Brian Kemp*

RCL2259 is run by The Kindness Offensive, a charity that believes in carrying out acts of kindness. Based in North London, the organisation won the Routemaster in a competition run by the White Stuff clothing company in 2010. As well as advertising, the bus transports people and goods to the location of the next act of kindness. This is the Strand in December 2013 but, when not running, the Kindbus can be found outside the former Aracataca Pub on Camden Road in Holloway. *Peter Horrex*

Epping & Ongar

Potter Street
Thornwood
Epping
North Weald

339

EPPING L.T. STATION

339

FISHPOOLS where furnishings a pleasure

KYY 527

The Epping & Ongar Railway is rapidly growing in popularity because of the 'across the board' nostalgia it provides. As well as operating steam and diesel trains on a section of the former Central Line from Ongar, there is a heritage bus link with today's Underground terminus at Epping.

An immaculate RT1700 arrives at the end of a run from Epping at The Two Brewers in Ongar. *Keith Valla*

A bus runs between Epping and North Weald every half-hour. On most weekends, eight services also run from North Weald to Epping and half continue to Shenfield railway station. RT3228 departs from Epping with RM216 waiting in the wings. *Keith Valla*

The heritage vehicles on the railway service are owned by The London Bus Company. On 30th March 2013, RT3238 and RT3871 wait at the stand near The Two Brewers pub before returning to Epping via North Weald. *Keith Valla*

RT1700 before departure from a rainy Shenfield on one of the four services linking the Epping & Ongar with the National Rail network.
Keith Valla

RT3871 provides some variety as it waits for passengers to emerge from the Underground at Epping. Incidentally, the E&OR is the nearest preserved line to central London.
Keith Valla

RT3228 is another regular performer. Here it's turning off Station Road into the drive leading to Epping station, past the iconic Underground sign.
Keith Valla

RTL1076 heads along the A414 while running from Ongar to Epping. This was one of eleven 'RT family' vehicles repatriated from Canada by Roger Wright's London Bus Company in May 2010. Abegweit Tours, based in Prince Edward Island, had bought them over a 20-year period from 1964. When the owner decided to sell up, LBC stepped in and shipped the whole lot back via Liverpool Docks. *Keith Valla*

In addition to the 339 service, there is a 381 on summer weekends and during special events on the railway. The route, normally operated by RFs, runs between North Weald and Epping but via Blake Hall and Toot Hill, taking in much more of the scenic Essex countryside. RF539 & RT3228 line up at North Weald station. *Keith Valla*

RM1966 makes a wonderful sight at Kelvedon Hatch, the well-known location of the 'secret' nuclear bunker. The bus is heading for Shenfield on the service from Epping. *Dave McKay*

A staged photograph? RT1700 heads into Ongar past RF539 without a driver because he's taking the photo. *Keith Valla*

RF180 near Blake Hall while working the 381 in August 2013. There are three trips each way on this route in the early afternoon. *Keith Valla*

A pool of around eight of LBC's extensive fleet is allocated to the Ongar services. Normally RF401 would be on the 381, but here impersonates a 339. It has stopped for photos on the A414 on the outskirts of Ongar. *Keith Valla*

You can find further details of the Epping & Ongar railway and bus operation on the website: *www.eorailway.co.uk*

Company Business

TIMEBUS TRAVEL
Classic London Buses
☎ 01727 866248

www.timebus.co.uk

WLT 450

The lure of an old London bus is too much to resist for many businesses, so there is a healthy hire market with corporates for all manner of promotional activity. Here, for instance, is Timebus's RM450, whose top deck haircut makes it ideal as a mobile TV studio. We think this is a shoot for the BBC's Blue Peter, endlessly circling Parliament Square. Kiddies on the pavement became very excited when they saw the presenter, although the photographer hadn't a clue who she was.
David Maxey

This evening job for Ensign called for RT4421, RT1431, RT8 and RT1499 to pick up in York Way, alongside King's Cross station, between 5.30 and 6.30pm. The passengers were a group of scientists visiting London for a conference and their destination aboard the buses was a restaurant on the South Bank. *Bob Stanger*

While waiting for the scientists to finish their meal, one of Ensign's staff noticed the indicator switch on RT8 had worked loose. With no repair facilities to hand, it was decided to return the bus to the depot as there was ample room on the remaining vehicles for the journey back to King's Cross.
RT8 was photographed on the Embankment before its return to Purfleet. *Bob Stanger*

Siemens hired RML2263 and RML2389 to take some of its customers from Rotherhithe to the London Eye. The vehicles park beside the wheel and County Hall. *Keith Valla*

In 2012 Ensign completed the painstaking restoration of its unique Leyland Cub, C4. M&G Investments hired the vehicle in 2013 for the week of the Chelsea Flower Show, which the company sponsored. Here's the bus en route to south-west London. *Bob Stanger*

Below: C4 ferries some M&G customers in Chelsea Bridge Road, along the side of the Flower Show site. *David Maxey*

Ensign won the contract to transfer the elite runners in the 2011 London marathon from their hotel to the start at Blackheath. RCL2220, RM1361, RML2405, RM25 and RMA50 await their special passengers on the north side of Tower Bridge. When the race begins, this is part of the route, hence the crowd barriers. The bus diversions are quite interesting too. *Bob Stanger*

After dropping off the runners at Blackheath, the RMs ran to the finish line in The Mall to collect the athletes afterwards. Not surprisingly the buses created a lot of interest with marathon spectators. RCL2220 is the subject of one of hundreds of cameras and camera phones.
Bob Stanger

ISIS Education provides English courses for foreign students as well as educational travel. Ensign's contract from the company in July 2013 involved not only supplying buses, but also conductors to act as tour guides on a trip around London. From left to right, RML2734, RCL2226, RML2588, ER882, RML2405 and RM25 stand by for a day of touring at Seagrove Road car park, Earls Court. *Christopher Rose*

A major Timebus job for the corporate market: RML2310, RM29, RML2263, RMA9, RML2442 and RML2389 are waiting at Millbank for the arrival of a boat conveying delegates to a tourist conference. From Millbank they were transported to Hurlingham Park. *Keith Valla*

In July 2013 a corporation needed seventeen RMs to transport staff and customers between the Grosvenor and Park Lane Hilton hotels to Tower Hill. A number of heritage bus operating companies supplied vehicles - Timebus, The London Bus Company, Traditional Travel, Dave's Buses and Red Bus. Tower Hill coach station in Lower Thames Street became a parking area before the return trips. From left to right, RMA37, RML2270, RM545, RML2301, RMC1477, unidentified, RML2527 and another RM. *Thomas Drake*

For a fashion event held in 2011 at two venues, Earls Court and London Olympia, Timebus ran a shuttle between the two. RML2263 and RML2389 stand on the forecourt at Earls Court before another journey to Olympia. *Keith Valla*

RMA9 leaves Earls Court on one of the shuttles. This bus was one of the coaches built for British European Airways in 1967, as BEA46. The fleet ran between the dedicated BEA terminal at Heathrow and a check-in facility in West Kensington. London Transport bought the vehicle in 1975 and it spent a year at Romford garage working route 175. In the background is RMC1477, whose lineage is completely different. *Keith Valla*

PREMIUM COACHES
www.premiumcoaches.co.uk
020 7713 1311

Harrods

WESTMINSTER TRAFALGAR SQUARE
THE LONDON EYE BIG BEN & MORE...

6

RM85

711 XUW

Central London is almost overrun by sightseeing buses, but only a few of the smaller operators use heritage vehicles. The word-famous Harrods store teamed up with Premium Tours to operate its own version for the tourists. RM85 at Trafalgar Square. *David Maxey*

RM85 was closed top for the winter months. In the summer, the partial open-toppers were more common. RM1979 treats its passengers to a slow pass of Downing Street, Whitehall government offices and Horse Guards Parade. *David Maxey*

RML2621's crew take a break outside St. James's Palace at the western end of Pall Mall in October 2013. *David Maxey*

According to Premium Tours' website, the Harrods bus has now been discontinued, but there are "new red bus tours coming soon".

Here's a couple of Premium's red Routemasters working sightseeing tours in different parts of London. RML2729 coasts along the St. Paul's end of Cannon Street. It was withdrawn by London United in 2004 and had spells as a sightseeing bus in Northern Ireland (where it was open-topped) and Dublin before returning to the capital. Premium acquired it in 2010. *David Maxey*

RML2348 used to be a Metroline bus based at Willesden. When new, it was allocated to London Country and worked local services in the Windsor and Slough area. This, however, is the Hyde Park Corner end of Piccadilly in April 2013. *Peter Horrex*

Ensignbus has linked up with Evans Evans tours to run a sightseeing trip with a World War 2 theme. A morning and an afternoon trip runs on Tuesday, Thursday and Saturday between April and October.
The morning tour focusses on the City of London and includes a visit to the National Army Museum. RT1499 at Aldwych. *Brian Kemp*

RTL453 at Trafalgar Square, a vehicle often pressed into service when demand is high. This RTL has had the roofbox body since 1962, when it was based at Shepherd's Bush garage working route 11. It was preserved in 1970 and passed to Ensign in 2010. *Brian Kemp*

RMA50 at the same spot. This one started life as BEA coach 34. It was bought by LT in 1979 and worked initially as a staff bus at Fulwell garage. For a time it was in the Stagecoach Scotland preserved fleet and also had a spell with Mac Tours in Edinburgh before Ensign acquired it in 2009. *Brian Kemp*

The beautifully-restored RT8 at the stand in Vauxhall Bridge Road before working the afternoon tour, taking in the Westminster area with an option to visit the Churchill War Rooms. *Ken Carr*

You could write a small book about RT8, but in very broad outline, it spent most of its original London life at the old garage by Putney Bridge, then a period as a trainer at a number of garages across the capital. After withdrawal, it was exported to the USA in 1960 and remained there for more than forty years before repatriation. Ensign's rebuilding of the vehicle has been well-documented; it re-emerged in 2010 and has been a regular performer on the Wartime Tour ever since.

Above: RT198 heads along Whitehall on an afternoon journey. For 2014 the tours are being rebranded under a Churchill's London banner. The morning trip, from Victoria, lasts for three & three-quarter hours and costs £24.00 for adults. The afternoon tour is £26.00, but you can book for both at a combined fare of £48.00. *David Maxey*

Below: The afternoon trip picks up and sets down at Victoria as well as the London Visitor Centre at Trafalgar Square. RT198 pulls away from the Whitehall stop. *Brian Kemp*

Premium's new tour in 2014 takes visitors to and up the Shard, London's tallest building. RM1979 has been redecorated with special vinyls for this work and here approaches Lambeth Palace. The tour runs on Tuesday, Thursday and Saturday. *David Maxey*

In the summer of 2013, the National Trust and Go-Coach put on a shuttle bus from Sevenoaks to the 15th century Knole House, at weekends and on Tuesday and Wednesday, with six trips each day. RML2699 arrives at Knole after completing another circular journey from Sevenoaks. *Ian Nightingale*

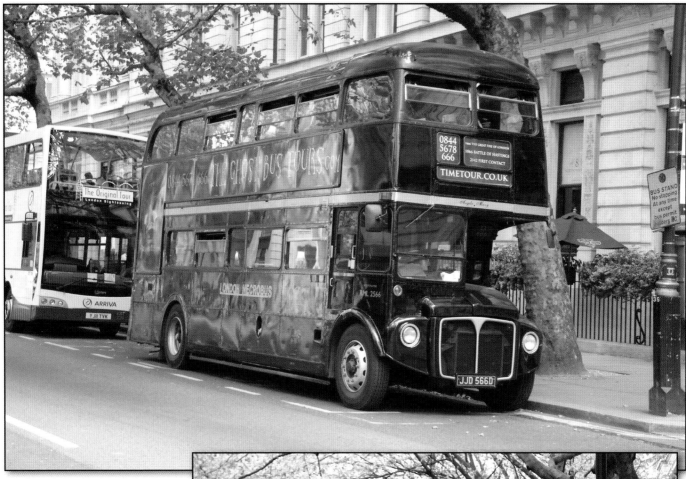

We round off with the Ghost Bus Tour operation in London. It runs every day with two departures at 7.30pm and 9pm. During daylight you can usually find the black Routemaster, RML2566, on a stand in Northumberland Avenue.
The tour is more deathly than ghostly, concentrating on locations where famous murders, executions and tortures took place. *Ken Carr*

Despite the content, the tour is light-hearted, with actors on board as guides. Curtains and table lamps inside the bus also add a certain ambience. A second vehicle ran in London until June 2013, RM1666. As you will see in a few pages time, it has migrated north. Here it is, in daylight again, at the Northumberland Avenue stand. *David Maxey*

The Edinburgh visit begins with ERM163 (RM163) working for Mac Tours at Waverley station. *Stuart Montgomery*

Mac Tours is a subsidiary of Lothian Buses and, as the name suggests, operates guided tours around Edinburgh. RCL2248, one of two RCLs in the fleet, awaits departure from the amphitheatre at the Our Dynamic Earth science centre. *Stuart Montgomery*

Routemasters operate the City Tour from the begining of April to the end of October. Every weekend, and daily during July and August, there is a fifteen minute frequency. For the rest of the operating period, it's every 20 minutes. RM90 stands on North Bridge above Waverley station. *Stuart Montgomery*

RM242 makes its away along the Royal Mile. The tour takes around an hour and in 2014 the fare is £14 for adults and £6 for children. You can hop on and hop off the buses if you desire and the ticket is valid for 24 hours.
Stuart Montgomery

RCL2248 waits to begin on Waverley Bridge. Mac Tours has ten RMs running alongside the RCLs and all have had haircuts, some more severe than others.
Stuart Montgomery

Earlier we saw black RM1666 on Ghost Tour duty in London. A month later, it turned up north of the border to work the new Edinburgh Ghost Bus Tour, where it also has a stand on Waverley bridge.

From Wednesday to Sunday the tour departs at 7.15pm with an additional trip at 9pm on Friday and Saturday. *Stuart Montgomery*

Scottish Travel's RML2697 sits outside St Michael's Parish Church in Slateford Road, Edinburgh, waiting for 75 wedding guests to board for a trip to the reception.

By all accounts, it was an eventful day: the bride turned up 45 minutes late and Stuart the photographer, who is also the musical director at the church, had to keep the congregation entertained with a much longer than expected organ recital. When it finally began, the wedding was Coca-Cola themed! Let's hope it hadn't gone flat by then.
Stuart Montgomery

The 2012 Scottish Cup Final was contested by Edinburgh's bitter rivals, Hearts and Hibs. Hearts won easily 5-1 and, next day, paraded the cup through the streets of the city aboard RM94, another of the Lothian Buses collection. *Stuart Montgomery*

Earlier you saw this bus, RCL2259, in its current guise working for the Kindness Offensive. Here it is with previous owners White Stuff, promoting the company's latest store opening in George Street, Edinburgh.

The vehicle has a removable roof, and you can just see the join of the centre section between the front and rear domes. *Stuart Montgomery*

Most of the companies operating London routes for TfL have held on to a small number of Routemasters, either for private hire or special events. Arriva is perhaps the most active with its branded Heritage Fleet but, like other operators, finds time to 'wave the flag' at enthusiast events. Here at the 2011 Showbus, for instance, is RM6, still wearing its Golden Jubilee paint. *David Maxey*

Although RM5 is privately-owned, it operates regularly as part of Arriva's special fleet. In this picture from December 2013, the bus is heading off to the crew's lunch break after decanting a party of ladies in Oxford Street for a spot of Christmas shopping. *David Maxey*

Arriva London North organised a day of road runs in July 2013 to celebrate the centenary of Tottenham Garage, allowing many of the types that had worked route 76 over the decades to appear again. An open-top RM was probably an anomaly but RMC1464 looked splendid amid the scrubbed stone of the City. This is Moorgate on an outward run to Waterloo. Funds raised from selling a souvenir programme went to a north London charity. *David Maxey*

Slightly closer cosmetically to route 76's former Routemasters is RM2217, here passing the distinctive No 1 Poultry on the running day. Although never a Tottenham bus (it started life at Willesden and finished up at Brixton), 2217 has two major claims to fame: it was the last of the standard length buses to be built and also the last, officially, to work a scheduled journey in London, on route 159 on December 9th 2005. (This is contentious; some say a different bus was the last RM on the road that day). The vehicle has also been on a round-Britain tour in purple as the Harry Potter 'Knight Bus', but without the third deck, obviously. *David Maxey*

There was a special gathering of RMCs at the London Bus Museum in October 2012 to mark the 50th anniversary of the type. The first of six to arrive were RMC1490 (normally to be found at the Crewe Heritage Centre) and RMC1453 (the Arriva RM coach without the haircut). 1453 was another of the last day runners on route 159. *David Maxey*

Another corporate outing for the Arriva Heritage Fleet in October 2012 involved three buses - RMC1453, RM2217, and this one, RM1124. The three spent a day shuttling back and forth between restaurants in Berkeley Street, North Audley Street and Sherwood Street (behind Piccadilly Circus) for a party of foodies during the London Restaurant Festival. This is RM2217 in Berkeley Street. *David Maxey*

Meanwhile back at the 76 running day, RML901 pulls away from the stop at the northern end of City Road. This is familiar territory for the bus as it once worked route 43 to London Bridge when based at the former Muswell Hill garage. How much of the original RML901 remains today . . . *David Maxey*

The Go-Ahead Commercial Services fleet undertakes similar one-off work as its Arriva counterpart, but also provides multiple vehicles at major events during the year. This is a one-off - RM9's appearance at the LBM's spring gathering in April 2013, which included a couple of 'route 462' trips around the Weybridge circuit, taking in the station, the war memorial, Waitrose, the library and Sullivans wine bar. *David Maxey*

Many of the Comm. Svcs. fleet reside at south London garages when not in use. This, for instance, is RML2604 taking a break at New Cross in 2011 alongside a newly-delivered batch of Enviro400s for the route 436 conversion. *David Maxey*

The major annual event for the division is the Wimbledon tennis fortnight when the shuttle buses from the station and park & ride sites often reach double figures. Heritage appears alongside more modern kit, like RML2472 struggling up Wimbledon Hill during the 2012 Championships. Outside the London area, Go-Ahead also provides transport for the Silverstone Grand Prix and the bi-annual Farnborough Air Show.   *David Maxey*

The Chelsea Flower Show is another fixed date in the calendar, although requiring fewer vehicles. RMs run alongside the gold-numbered Presidents between Victoria station and the Royal Hospital site. Here's RML2520 setting off along Buckingham Palace Road in May 2011.   *David Maxey*

The open-top RML in the Go-Ahead fleet, 2318, is finished in a sort-of London General Omnibus Company scheme. You may have seen it on local telly in the south-east at the start of 2014, taking part in the victory parade for Olympic gold medallist Lizzy Yarnold. This, however, is a slightly more mundane shuttle from Victoria to the 'flahs' in 2013. *David Maxey*

Finally, let us not forget Metroline, which has a couple of vehicles available for similar hire - the open-top RM644 and RML903. Here they both are at Holloway garage open day in 2011. In March 2013, RML903 ran several return journeys on route 4, taking donations for Red Nose Day instead of fares. The Commissioner's RM1005 was similarly engaged on route 24. *David Maxey*

CONGRATULATIONS
ON YOUR
WEDDING DAY

WLT 516

The popularity of heritage buses with the general public is very good news for owners, especially if they have spare time at weekends when weddings tend to happen. These days, demand is huge, not least because one bus may be able to carry the entire wedding party from church to reception, allowing both families to mingle fraternally before drink enters the picture (the real reason, of course, is that traffic and parking cease to be an issue).

A host of private operators provide vehicles to this market, as well as the much larger companies like Go-Ahead. DRM2516 waits for guests to board outside the RAF church of St Clement Danes. *David Maxey*

The privately-owned RML2382 on wedding duty in April 2013, passing the Tower of London. The route 19 blinds it usually displays are a throwback to its final service with Arriva at Brixton garage, where it worked the last day of crew operation on the route in 2005. *David Maxey*

A fully-loaded RML2516 pulls away from Windsor Parish Church in the High Street while on loan to Travel With Hunny in May 2012. Later that year, Ensign hired it, then bought it, before passing it on again to Ghost Bus Tours in 2013. If anyone would care to unravel the mechanical connections between this vehicle and DRM2516 (with special reference to RML2283), please go ahead. *David Maxey*

From the numberplate this is RML2322 although, frankly, it could be anything. Sticking with the original premise, 2322 started life with London Country at Northfleet. It was repainted red in 1980 for London Sovereign, finished its service career at Tottenham and has been privately-owned since 2005. Here it's waiting for a wedding party in Upper Montagu Street, across the road from Marylebone Register Office. *David Maxey*

RML2374, showing a route 19 blind for no good historical reason (it was a First Group bus post-deregulation), crosses Waterloo Bridge in July 2012. Before it was bought privately in 2007, the vehicle worked First's park & ride journeys in Plymouth. *David Maxey*

The London Bus Company's RML897 passes King's Cross while heading to the very busy Marylebone Manacling Centre. The unlovely turquoise paint of the former station frontage has now been swept away and the original open piazza re-created. How long before they start digging it up again? *Peter Horrex*

This is stylish; not even the royals have RMs when they tie the knot at the Abbey. Timebus provided two vehicles for this Westminster event - RML2389 and RML2527. Lovely day for it too. *Keith Valla*

RML2278 rounds Aldwych in July 2012. This one started life at Tottenham, then Chalk Farm on route 24, but became another First Bus at deregulation. It's been in private hands since 2004 and now works for Thisbus alongside five other RMLs in the company's hire fleet. There are histories of all six on the website: www.thisbus.com *David Maxey*

Traditional Travel of Bromley has five RMLs and an open-top RM. RML2301 at Marble Arch in May 2013 shows off the usual trimmings the company deploys. This was another Chalk Farm bus in the early 1970s, but it finished its career with Arriva at Brixton. *David Maxey*

The Timebus base at South Mimms, with five of the thirteen-strong Routemaster fleet waiting for wedding bells. Left to right, RML2442, RML2263, RMC1477, RMA37 and RML2389. There's also three RLHs and an RF, which will appear shortly. *Ken Carr*

Ensign's ER882 at the Angel, Islington. This was one of twenty-four built in 1961 with an extra bay and seventy-two seats, extending the length to thirty feet. When a later batch of 500 began rolling off the production line, the Extended Routemasters were re-lettered as RMLs. *Peter Horrex*

Ensign's RML2683 pitches up at Clapham Junction. In the background is the Arding & Hobbs department store , now masquerading as a Debenhams.

The Enviro, E112, is one of twenty-nine dedicated vehicles based at Camberwell for route 345.   *David Maxey*

RML2310 arrives at the Harcourt Arms in Marylebone and joins SRM7 (RM1871) to await the end of a wedding at the nearby Swedish Church. Both vehicles were supplied by Timebus.

RM1871 has been with the company since 1997 and, since then, has carried the silver scheme applied in 1977 to celebrate the first Jubilee.
Keith Valla

A lovely springtime shot of RML2527 awaiting guests in Denham. This one went new to Upton Park in 1966 for route 15, but also served at Holloway, Edgware and Bow. It spent its final year at Tottenham for Arriva and was bought by Timebus in 2005.   *Keith Valla*

RMC1477 outside Hackney Town Hall in July 2011. Sixty-eight standard length Routemaster Coaches entered service from 1962 on Green Line services. They had wider-spaced seats with deeper upholstery, reducing the number to 57. They also were fitted with semi-automatic gearboxes with revised ratios to allow higher speeds, as opposed to the automatic boxes on standard RMs. *Keith Valla*

Although the wedding circuit is dominated by Routemasters, you do find other types. Here, RLH23 joins RML2389 at Syon House. The London RLHs entered service from 1950; essentially, they were lowbridge RTs, but not nearly as pretty. *Keith Valla*

RLH61 at Vange, Essex. The Weymann body shape was similar to the pre-war STL, hence the lack of sophistication, but serious nostalgics are more likely to remember the side gangway on the top deck which intruded onto the lower deck. Seventy-six were built in two batches and worked in both the central and country areas. *Bob Stanger*

For those with fewer friends and family, an RF is just the job. Timebus's RF491 waits outside Christ Church in East Sheen before taking the guests to Pembroke Lodge in Richmond Park. *Keith Valla*

Finally, a couple of shots from St Paul's Cathedral. Above: RF491 takes on a central London assignment.
Below: A much grander affair, needing the carrying capacity of RM450,

RM545 and RM479. Two things to admire here: 1. the optimism of going for a pair of open-tops. 2. How it's possible for two people to have so many friends. Both *Keith Valla*

A Secret Reserve

On February 5th & 6th 2014, the RMT union held a two-day Underground strike to protest against the proposed closure of ticket offices. To help keep the capital moving, TfL called on bus operators far and wide to provide extra vehicles, turning parts of London into a heritage rally. London Bus Company's RML897 was allocated to rush-hour trips on route 29 and parked in Northumberland Avenue between the peaks. *David Maxey*

Stagecoach's RM324 was pressed into service on route 158. Here it's heading along Leyton High Road with all its lights on, highlighting the miserable weather conditions endured on the second day of the strike.
Ken Carr

Route 25 enjoyed a mixture of old and new from Ensignbus, providing extra cover from Stratford into central London. RT3232 waits for the afternoon rush hour to begin at the Stratford City bus station.   *Christopher Rose*

Later in the day, RT3232 takes a breather at Holborn before heading back to Stratford. A packed VN36134, one of the regular allocation, makes for the route's usual destination, Ilford. Even without a strike, route 25 is the busiest in London, carrying more than 23 million passengers a year. *Christopher Rose*

With the extra buses running mainly in rush hour, somewhere had to be found for park them during the day. This is Camden Road in Holloway, where LBC's RT3062, RML899 and RM298 found refuge before heading back to Trafalgar Square on Day Two. *Albert Dawson*

Normally you would find a line of nearly-new Volvo hybrids parked here between route 29 journeys. Strike days, however, produced another re-creation of the 1960s in Northumberland Avenue. This is literally 'across the road' from Trafalgar Square. *David Maxey*

RM1361 was one of the route 38 extras and is here on the final leg of its journey at Piccadilly Circus. Seven or eight RMs from Ensign and Timebus appeared on the 38 on the second day. Soon after this shot was taken, the statue of Eros was covered up for building work to begin (very unusual to find building work in London), so failed to appear in the route 22 running day photos two months later. *David Maxey*

At Victoria, part of the route 38 collection stabled in Vauxhall Bridge Road before starting return journeys at around 3.30. *David Maxey*

A second strike was called on 29th & 30th April 2014, bringing RML2679 into action on route 8 between Bow and Liverpool Street. The RML has just moved off the stand in Bevis Marks at the start of a journey back to Bow. *Ken Carr*

RTs worked extra turns on route 15 during the second strike. Above: RT3251 negotiates the Trafalgar Square roundabout on a return run to Blackwall. *Albert Dawson*

Like the first strike, routes 29 and 38 enjoyed the highest number of heritage vehicles on the extras. Right: RMA50 sets off from Victoria. Below: RT3238 in Tottenham Court Road on a short run to Holloway Nag's Head. Both *Albert Dawson*

For The Enthusiast

Kennington Brixton
Streatham Norbury
Thornton Heath Pond
Croydon

STOCKWELL GARAGE

SERVICE J
CIRCULAR TOUR
OF LONDON

STOCKWELL GARAGE

RTL453

RTL1076

KLB648

LUC253

With so much interest in London's heritage buses, it's not surprising that regular events are laid on for the enthusiast, in the form of tours, route re-creations and running days. The Classic London Bus Society's tours provide excellent entertainment, including photo stops during the day. From one such trip, here's RTL453 and RTL1076 posing inside Stockwell garage.
Bob Stanger

Another TCLBS tour featured both of Ensignbus's Cravens-bodied RTs, the only two now in existence. The tour began from Victoria Coach Station and headed north to cover routes in the Harrow and Watford areas. RT1499 & RT1431 get ready for the 'off'.
Bob Stanger

The two buses inside the coach station, with inevitable white jobs. When new, RT1499, on the right, was allocated to the LT garage in Gillingham Street, Victoria, where you can now find a Sainsbury's. That's progress.
Bob Stanger

In August 2010 the TCLBS hired the newly-restored RT8 to retrace the original route 30. As a bonus, the organisers arranged for RT1 to meet up with RT8 at Putney Heath, not far from the Green Man bus stand.
Bob Stanger

RF600 parked in Gillingham Street in September 2013 before the start of a two-day road run visiting the site of every London Country garage that once had an RF allocation. The area south of London was tackled on the first day; the vehicle stabled at Brooklands overnight and then headed north, rounding off with yet another supermarket in Epping.
David Maxey

On 9th February 2014, TCLBS headed south of the river to re-create two tram replacement routes and to visit Plumstead garage. RTL139 and RTL453 were deployed this time. This is 453 near Brockley station.
Christopher Rose

The route 213 RF commemoration on 2nd December 2012 produced multiple red vehicles between Kingston/New Malden and Sutton garage, running a planned15-minute interval service. It was so like the real thing (especially when three came along at once), it was almost worth freezing one's wotsits. This is RF368 in Malden Road, Worcester Park.
David Maxey

The actual 60th anniversay of red RF introduction was celebrated, to the day, on 11th September 2012, with up to eight vehicles running on route 210 between Finsbury Park and Golders Green. This is RF433 in the Archway one-way. To add extra character, TD95 joined in as well. *David Maxey*

A number of Country Area running days take place each year and there are two main organisers of these enjoyable events.
In May 2013, Amersham & District Motorbus Society (ADMS) added a new running day at Harlow. GS13 has just arrived at The Green Man stop in Old Harlow.
Thomas Drake

BN45, one of the diminutive Bristol LHs, arrives at Harlow bus station. This one transferred to Harlow from Leatherhead in February 1977 and stayed until a move to Grays in September 1979.
Thomas Drake

Five RTs also took part in the 2013 event. From left to right, RT1499, RT3254, RT3232, RT2083 and RT1700 pose for the cameras at Harlow bus station.
Keith Valla

The ADMS running day at Slough celebrates its 10th anniversary in June 2014. From the 2010 event, this is STL441 heading for Beaconsfield and passing the building work for the new Slough bus station.
Keith Valla

Buses head out to all points of the compass at the Slough event. In May 2012, RT2083 is going to Pinewood Studios on the Uxbridge Road near Black Park. Close behind, RML2428 is bound for Uxbridge.
David Maxey

The Church of St John the Baptist in Windsor High Street appears for a second time in the book as RTL139 motors past.
This is another journey that started from Slough.
David Maxey

All three of these are from the 2013 East Grinstead running day, an annual event organised by Country Bus Rallies.
From the top, GS34 and RF679 meet up at Dormansland; experimental Atlantean XF3 is about to set off from East Grinstead High Street, and
SNB340 enjoys the early spring weather at Crawley Down.
As research has shown, even Leyland Nationals are regarded as heritage by a certain generation.
David Maxey

Although not as big as some events, the North London Transport Society's Theydon Bois gatherings do provide the sight of heritage buses running through Epping Forest. On its way to the April 2013 event, Ensign's Leyland Cub, C4, re-created route 381 between Toothill and Epping. *Thomas Drake*

RF319 arrives in Theydon Bois only a few yards from the Village Hall, the starting point for the road trips and where you will find the transport bazaar. *Thomas Drake*

Opposite: Strictly speaking, trips start from the car park, which becomes a bus station for the day. An RML has arrived from Epping just before DMS2357 heads out on its own journey. *David Maxey*

In March 2012, a special running day commemorated 40 years since the withdrawal of route 336A between Rickmansworth and Loudwater Village. The village is now a private estate and entry is normally only allowed to residents. GS64 and GS13 were the buses chosen to visit this exclusive enclave. *Thomas Drake*

As well as the Loudwater visit, the chance was taken to draft in T792 to run along routes 309 and 361. The AEC Regal is about to depart from Chorleywood on the run back to Rickmansworth. *Thomas Drake*

Another of Country Bus Rallies' annual events is held at Hertford. RF539 overtakes RW3 outside Hertford station while on a trip to Old Harlow. The RW class was an experiment; three were built in1960 and they worked in the London area for only three years. RW3 spent its last year at Hertford. *Thomas Drake*

Every one of these running days has a wide range of vehicles for visitors to enjoy. Hertford's selection in June 2013 included RT604 in National Bus Company light green. This one is a regular at running events in the Home Counties, and here departs from Hertford station. *Albert Dawson*

The Amersham & District Motorbus Society's Uxbridge running day appears to have been cancelled for 2014. These two photos provide a comparison between the Green Line-dedicated RT3254 and workaday country bus RML2440. Both are approaching Uxbridge. *Thomas Drake*

Country Bus Rallies holds an event in Sevenoaks each May, centred around the bus station. In 2013 RML2699 adds a rare splash of red. The majority of buses attending these events tend to be in variations of country area green livery, for the sake of local accuracy if nothing else. *Albert Dawson*

GS2 gives it some revs on a trip from Sevenoaks to Dunton Green. Not quite Euro-6, is it? *Albert Dawson*

The 9th Hemel Hempstead event will be held in August 2014, another one organised by Amersham & District. After working from Hemel, RF539 poses at journey's end outside the former Ovaltine factory at Kings Langley. The space now accommodates flats, but the original facade has been restored. *Keith Valla*

RT3254 swings into Hemel Hempstead bus station with a trip from Welwyn Garden City at the 2012 event. This privately-owned bus is another regular on the running day scene. *Keith Valla*

Not surprisingly, the first ADMS event was held in Amersham and continues into its 26th year in 2014. RT4779 takes a tight turn on Chesham Broadway while running from Windsor to Berkhampstead.
Keith Valla

A rather stunning contrast between red RF and rebuilt Green Line version in Beaconsfield during the 2013 Amersham event. Central area RF453 is working a Beaconsfield to Penn service and passing the photographer's recently acquired RF281. *Keith Valla*

Metroline's annual garage open day at Potters Bar always attracts a good selection of London heritage buses, many of which take visitors on trips around the area. The aforementioned Leyland Tiger, TD95, heads back to the garage at South Mimms. *Thomas Drake*

The M25 motorway provides the backdrop at South Mimms as RMC1486 returns to Potters Bar after a run to St. Albans. *Albert Dawson*

Canada

BIG Pink Sightseeing

Gray Line

CHARTER THIS BUS
423-6242
ANTIQUEBUS.COM

Gray Line

Durty Nelly's
An Authentic Irish Pub

GUINNESS

RML 2328

ROUTEMASTER
RML 2328

A

NOVA SCOTIA
17·671·D
COMMERCIAL

CUV 328C

Outside Britain, Eastern Canada is the hotspot for working
Routemasters. Two companies operate large fleets,
Double-Deck Tours and Absolute Charters. Absolute's

RML2328 takes its turn on the sightseeing tour around
Halifax, Nova Scotia. *Wilson Hum*

The Absolute Charter fleet is used for City tours, private hire and ferrying cruise ship passengers from the port of Halifax into the city. As you can see, the company's vehicles are a colourful bunch. RML2309, RML2677, RML881, RML2328, RML2314, RML2578 and RM937 line up at their base in Mackintosh Street, Halifax. *Wilson Hum*

Absolute's Fleet

	Acquired
RML881	**2005**
RM937	**2005**
RM1018	**2011**
RML2281	**2010**
RML2309	**2009**
RML2314	**2006**
RML2316	**2005**
RML2328	**2010**
RML2329	**2005**
RML2332	**2006**
RML2336	**2010**
RML2365	**2009**
RML2373	**2005**
RML2465	**2009**
RML2507	**2006**
RML2525	**2009**
RML2534	**2009**
RML2553	**2009**
RML2578	**2006**
RML2651	**2010**
RML2664	**2005**
RML2673	**2006**
RML2675	**2009**
RML2677	**2009**
RML2689	**2009**

RML2677 appears on the Big Blue Bus tour, taking in Halifax's Pier 21, the waterfront and Citadel Hill. *Wilson Hum*

The Big Pink Sightseeing tour is a hop-on, hop-off service. RM937 is appropriately adorned for the working . *Wilson Hum*

Absolute has a staggering twenty-five Routemasters, and all bar two are RMLs. RM937, RML2328, RML2316, RML2336 and RML 2465 await their next jobs at the company HQ. *Paul Bateson*

Double Deck Tours is based in Niagara Falls, Ontario. The primary operation is sightseeing trips to the famous waterfall using a fleet of thirteen RMs. The fleet is also available for private hire and weddings. RM1618 and RM1242 await their next trips at the Bossert Road garage located about six miles from the city. *Paul Bateson*

DD's Fleet	
	Fleet No.
RM797	*17*
RM1102	*19*
RM1242	*08*
RM1604	*18*
RM1618	*10*
RM2162	*14*
RM2165	*04*
RM2206	*07*
RCL2252	*02*
RCL2255	*01*
RML2467	*24*
RML2501	*15*
RML2555	*23*

A better view of RM1242. Note that the route blinds match the vehicle's DD fleet number. *Paul Bateson*

RM1102 waits for its passengers to return at Table Rock - some of the 8 million people who visit the Falls each year. There's a visitor centre at Table Rock and observation decks at the foot of the Falls. *Paul Bateson*

RML2467 at Table Rock. This one has gone against convention - its route number doesn't match its fleet number, 24. And shouldn't that destination read Queen's Park? *Paul Bateson*

In Toronto, Bus & Boat Tours operates nine RMs. RM1651 was bought from Double-Deck Tours in 2006 (it was number 3 while in Niagara) and here stands in Shuter Street, Toronto. The other RMs in the fleet are RM504, RM727, RM1158, RM1676, RM1888, RM1909, RM2209 and RM2210. *Paul Bateson*

Another of the Bus & Boat fleet in June 2013, RM2209 is about to set off from Dundas Square, Toronto with a sightseeing trip. This bus was also bought from Double Deck Tours. *Paul Bateson*

Private Hire

You don't have to get married to hire a heritage bus. Any cause for celebration provides the perfect excuse, or a simple desire for a day out with a difference. Our first example is a birthday; RF401 heads along Victoria Embankment after dropping off Roger and his friends and family on the occasion of his 70th. *David Maxey*

RT1499 besides the Thames at Henley. This trip was organised for a group of friends who fancied the aforementioned different day out. Both organiser and driver/photographer are heavily involved in the Classic London Bus Society Tours we saw earlier. So you could also describe this as a busman's holiday.
Bob Stanger

The Timebus RF you saw in the wedding section also appears across London on non-nuptial-related events. In this shot, RF491 provides an ancient & modern contrast at Victoria while carrying a private party in June 2011. The ultra-modern building is known simply as 100 Victoria Street. *David Maxey*

RM479 in Hampstead while on private hire duty. According to the blind, Louise and Oliver are on tour. Whatever can that mean? *Keith Valla*

RF491 again, this time ferrying a group of sixteen-year-old pupils from Hyde Heath to their prom at the Uplands Hotel in High Wycombe. *Keith Valla*

Another school prom. This time RML2634 is transporting pupils to the 2013 event at the Thomas Alleyne school in Stevenage. *Albert Dawson*

We end the section with RT624 and another day out with a difference. At the start of it, the driver's instructions were to drive to Primrose Hill and call a mobile phone number. A man and his son then appeared with hampers of food and loaded them onto the bus. He explained that he planned to surprise his new fiancée, who duly turned up with her mother.

The first stop was Charing Cross station where, just after the photo was taken, 20-30 friends appeared. Next, Runnymede, by the river Thames, where two police riders flagged down the driver after he crossed their path into the car park so that passengers could get off briefly.

The man who'd hired the bus, acting as conductor for the day, spoke to the police and told the driver he was delaying the Queen on her way to Royal Ascot!

The day's final destination, Windsor, was less eventful. Here's RT624 mingling with the regular tourist buses. *Bob Stanger*

999

Doctor on Board
Serious Trauma Care 24/7
We are a Charity

LONDON'S AIR AMBULANCE

AIR AMBULANCE
WE NEED YOUR HELP

IMPALED ON RAILING
KENSINGTON

CONDITION: PENETRATING CHEST INJURY, UNCONSCIOUS, NO PULSE.
TREATMENT: OPEN HEART SURGERY, BLOOD TRANSFUSION.
RESPONSE TIME: 6 MINUTES.
OUTCOME: FULL RECOVERY.

LONDON'S AIR AMBULANCE

ALD 933B

This section includes all the photos that don't fit the earlier categories and reveals just how many different uses old London buses are put to. Charity involvement is high on the list, such as here in Trafalgar Square in September 2012 when Stagecoach provided RM1933 as a 'hospitality suite' for a fund-raising event in aid of the London Air Ambulance. Luckily the weather was much kinder on Day Two. *David Maxey*

The catering world loves Routemasters for some reason, although purists may need the smelling salts after looking at some of these pictures.

RML892 is used as an overspill for a cafe at Timmermans Garden Centre at Woodborough in Nottingham. *Derrick Yates*

On page 18 RCL2250 appeared in its previous incarnation, so here's how it looks now in Devon. On The Green, based in Kingsbridge, use it as a mobile cafe and it's often to be found at Paignton Zoo. This, though, is the Torquay Festival. *On The Green*

Over in Canada, RM1448 is a chip shop, but not a mobile chip shop. These two photos show the additions to the bus when it was converted to its new role in Manotick, Ontario. Why didn't Routemaster coaches have substantial doors like this? *Paul Bateson*

RT3593 originally worked at Niagara Falls for Double-Deck Tours. It's had a chequered life since. Here's the bus in Hamilton, Ontario, just before it reopened as a refreshment vehicle in 2013.
Paul Bateson

This RML appears to be a pub, unless the signage is wrong. RML2416 has been converted into a mobile drinks cabinet, branded as the 'Hop On Inn' (groan). Here, it's open for business at Meyrick Park in Bournemouth.
Justin Saunders

The famous Knight Bus from the Harry Potter movie *The Prisoner of Azkaban* can now be found at the Warner Bros studio in Leavesden, near Watford. The triple-decker was created using bodies from three different RTs, believed to be RT2240, RT3882 and RT4497. The combined bodywork now stands on a Dennis Javelin chassis. *Ken Carr*

RM577 was used by Waste Care, a waste management and recyling service, as a promotional tool, and a prize, at the RWM trade show held at the NEC

Birmingham in 2013. The lucky winner from Nottingham University won a day out for himself and 60 colleagues/students on the bus. *Ian Nightingale*

Camden Bus Estate Agent uses RT2157 as its office in Arlington Road, Camden. The bus sits snugly between two buildings and has had an entrance foyer built around the open platform. *Marcus Dawson*

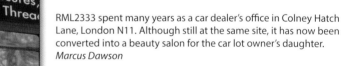

RML2333 spent many years as a car dealer's office in Colney Hatch Lane, London N11. Although still at the same site, it has now been converted into a beauty salon for the car lot owner's daughter. *Marcus Dawson*

RML2262 has a slightly bizarre new career. It works for a funeral company called A.W. Lymn in Nottingham and is available as either a hearse or for carrying passengers to the service. The inset shows a hoarding advertising this unique method of despatch. *Derrick Yates*

RML2710 was hired by the TSSA union to make a political statement on the day of the first 'Borismaster' public journey on route 38. The RML followed the brand-new LT2 all the way from Hackney to Victoria, doing its utmost to grab the attention of the media covering the event. Here, it's pulled up alongside the LT in Vauxhall Bridge Road after the new vehicle was taken out of service while 'software issues' were addressed. *Albert Dawson*

To celebrate the arrival of the re-created 'Winton Train' from Prague at Liverpool Street station, RT4421, RT1431, RT1 and STL2377 were lined up to await those on board, thus re-enacting a scene from 1939 when almost 700 Czechoslovak children were rescued by Sir Nicholas Winton and brought to Britain. *Bob Stanger*

On a different occasion at Liverpool Street, RM1005, owned by TfL Commissioner Sir Peter Hendy, provided support and transport on London Poppy Day in November 2012. This is a cash collection stop by members of the Armed Forces during a day-long tour of the capital. *David Maxey*

In November 2013, RM1005 raised funds for the annual Poppy Appeal by working route 211 for a day. This is one of the later journeys pulling away from Waterloo station. TfL Commissioner Sir Peter Hendy loaned his bus to the event and it was driven by a retired member of TfL staff who maintains his PCV licence. *Russell Young*

Metroline's RML903 at St George's Square, Pimlico, during the route 24 running day in November 2012 to mark its centenary. Although these events don't collect fares as such, passengers are expected to buy a souvenir programme whose proceeds go to a charity favoured by the bus operator. *David Maxey*

The slightly jaw-dropping sight of RML2263 and RML2389 standing on the forecourt of Buckingham Palace. They were being used to publicise tourism in the capital, ironically on the day of an Underground strike. Who says Londoners don't have a sense of humour? The second and third photos show RML2389 leaving through the Palace gates. *Keith Valla*

Heritage Route 9, or 9H, also began operating in November 2005 and originally ran from Aldwych (like the regular 9) to the Royal Albert Hall. The route was adjusted to run from Trafalgar Square to Kensington High Street in 2010 at the request of Kensington Council. RM1204 emerges from the stand in Great Scotland Yard. *David Maxey*

Route 9's Routemasters are based at Westbourne Park garage. Half the allocation, of ten, await their next turns in the garage yard. From left to right, SRM3 (RM1650), RM1562, RM1776 and RM1627. In the background, far right, is RM1640. *Danny Dudziec.*

RM1627 approaches the Royal Albert Hall on Kensington Gore, named after the Gore Estate which once owned the land. Opposite page: RM1204 stands over a maintenance pit at Westbourne Park.
Both *David Maxey*

We always refer to this as two icons for the price of one: The 5,272-seat Royal Albert Hall, completed in 1871, contrasted with the 64-seat RM1913, completed in 1964. If you'd like to take your own photo, a small red job passes the big red job every fifteen minutes. *David Maxey*

One Mayor's bright idea lines up alongside the next Mayor's bright idea. The two heritage routes were introduced by Ken Livingstone, partly to dilute criticism of the impending demise of Routemasters on scheduled services. The Boris bikes are the brainchild of the current Mayor. This is the junction of Kensington High Street with Kensington Church Street. On the left are the former Derry & Toms and Barkers department stores. *David Maxey*

Route 9, and especially the 9H section, has been called the least expensive sight-seeing tour in London as it passes so many iconic locations. Here's the leafy surroundings of Hyde Park Corner, with RM1640 heading into Piccadilly. *David Maxey*

RM1562 on the south side of the Hyde Park Corner roundabout, with Constitution Hill in the background. When First Group sold its London bus operation in 2013, the west London garages at Westbourne Park and Atlas Road were bought by the Australian-owned Tower Transit, who automatically inherited the 9H and its RMs. The gold First Group logo has now given way to a gold version of the Tower logo. *David Maxey*

RM1913, under Tower ownership in November 2013, approaches the roundabout from Piccadilly. The impressive Bomber Command Memorial was opened by HM The Queen in 2012. So, despite its heritage look, the RMs predate the new construction by some fifty years. *David Maxey*

RM1913 pulls away from its final stop in Cockspur Street next to Trafalgar Square in August 2012. This photo was taken fifteen months before the one above, yet the bus is carrying the same advertising. The backdrop here continues to be Canada House. *Ken Carr*

RM1735 begins the very cheap London sight-seeing tour by navigating the southern side of the Trafalgar Square islands. *David Maxey*
When the stand in Great Scotland Yard is full, heritage vehicles recess in Cockspur Street, which is also their first stop westbound. As we go to press, GSY is severely restricted by building work (very unusual to see building work in London), so the 9Hs may not return to the traditional stand (see below).

RM1005 made a guest appearance on Route 9 for a few days in the spring of 2014. The bus is based at Westbourne Park and is on Tower Transit's insurance policy. One of the drivers asked if he could use it for a day, and ended up using it for a whole week. On 1st April, 1005 pulls out of Scotland Place at the start of another trip to Kensington. *Keith Valla*

All this will come to an end in July 2014 when TfL withdraws the 9H's £1million annual subsidy. Apparently, the vehicles will be compared with the Stagecoach fleet and the best examples retained for the 15H. So, expect some withdrawals and some cannibalisation.

Until the 9Hs finish, there is this possibility to entertain you. The introduction in early February 2014 of silver-liveried 'Borismaster' LT150 on the regular route 9 provided the opportunity to photograph it with the silver SRM3. Although LT150 is due to move to route 10 (converted to LTs on 26/4/14), you will still be able to see both silver machines running alongside each other between Kensington and Hyde Park Corner station. The first picture shows the pair at the 9H's Warwick Gardens stand. *David Maxey*

The second was taken at the Trafalgar Square traffic lights beside Canada House. *Danny Dudziec*